FLORA & FAUNA

AN ILLUSTRATED ABC BOOK

FROM THE STUDENTS OF
COLUMBUS COLLEGE OF ART AND DESIGN

COLUMBUS COLLEGE OF ART & DESIGN
60 Cleveland Avenue, Columbus, OH 43215

Flora & Fauna: An Illustrated ABC Book
ISBN: 978-1503347090

Illustrations and text © 2013
by the Columbus College of Art & Design.
All rights reserved.

Book design by Trevor Payne. Project coordination and
direction by Adam Osgood and Rebecca Zomchek.

The illustrations in this book were created by the
students of *Illustration for Graphic Design*, taught
by Rebecca Zomchek and Adam Osgood.

Columbus College of Art & Design prepares tomorrow's creative leaders for
professional careers. With a history of commitment to fundamentals and quality,
CCAD advances a distinct, challenging, and inclusive learning culture that supports
individual development in art, design, and the humanities.

Columbus College of Art & Design
60 Cleveland Avenue, Columbus, OH 43215

www.ccad.edu

A message from the designer:

*This book is dedicated to all the CCAD friends and
faculty I've had the pleasure of working with.*

*Special thanks goes out to my family for the
never ending support and love.*

☙

Trevor Payne is an upperclassman at CCAD and designed
this book as a special project. His assignment included look
development, layout, image-editing, color-correction,
and custom hand-written typography.

"Geometry can produce legible letters but art alone makes them beautiful. Art begins where geometry ends, and imparts to letters a character transcending mere measurement."

–Paul Standard

This book is a collection of Drop Cap designs from the Columbus College of Art and Design's "Illustration for Graphic Design" Class of 2013. The class is designed to introduce graphic design students to the power of visual storytelling and expose them to the process of picture making from the perspective of an illustrator. Hand lettering is a fantastic example of the beautiful harmony that can work between traditional drawing skills and graphic design.

Our students were challenged to illustrate Drop Cap* designs in the theme of "Flora and Fauna," deriving inspiration from the natural world of plants and animals. These natural forms contrasted against the traditionally clean geometry found in typefaces forced the student-designers to think out of the box of standard type decoration.

This is Columbus College of Art and Design's first printed collection of the Drop Cap project, and the students have put together an excellent compendium of work showcasing multiple visual styles and artistic problem solving. We hope to continue this tradition and level of design work for years to come.

–Rebecca Zomchek & Adam Osgood
Assistant Professors, Illustration Department, CCAD

*Drop Cap: In book publishing the first letter of a paragraph that is enlarged to "drop" down two or more lines, as in the next paragraph. Drop caps are often seen at the beginning of novels, where the top of the first letter of the first word lines up with the top of the first sentence and drops down to the four or fifth sentence to the beginning of a section (webopedia.com). Or: A large, often highly decorated letter set at the beginning of a chapter, verse, or paragraph (thefreedictionary.com).

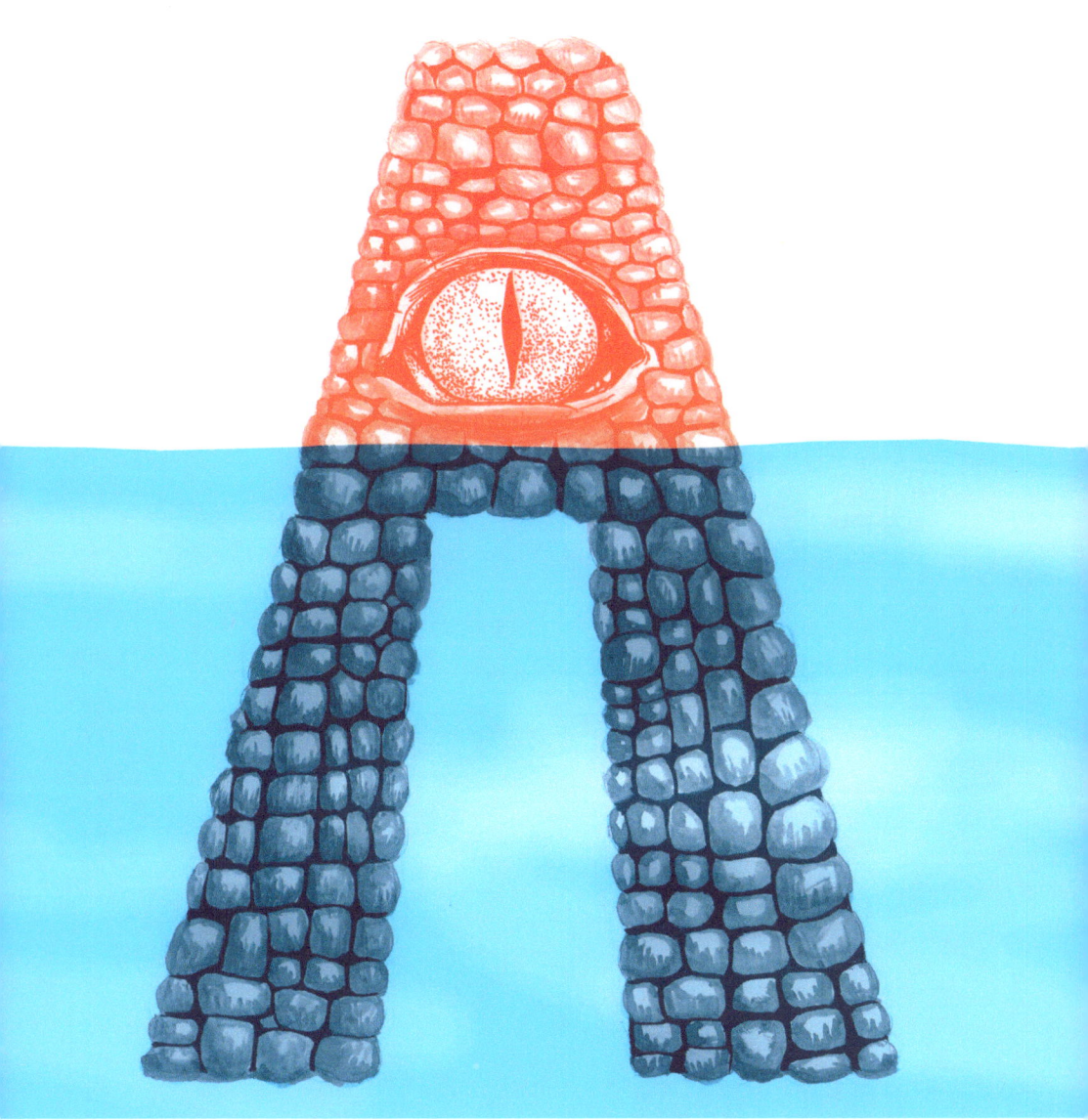

*A*LLIGATOR

Candice Oates
coates.1@go.ccad.edu

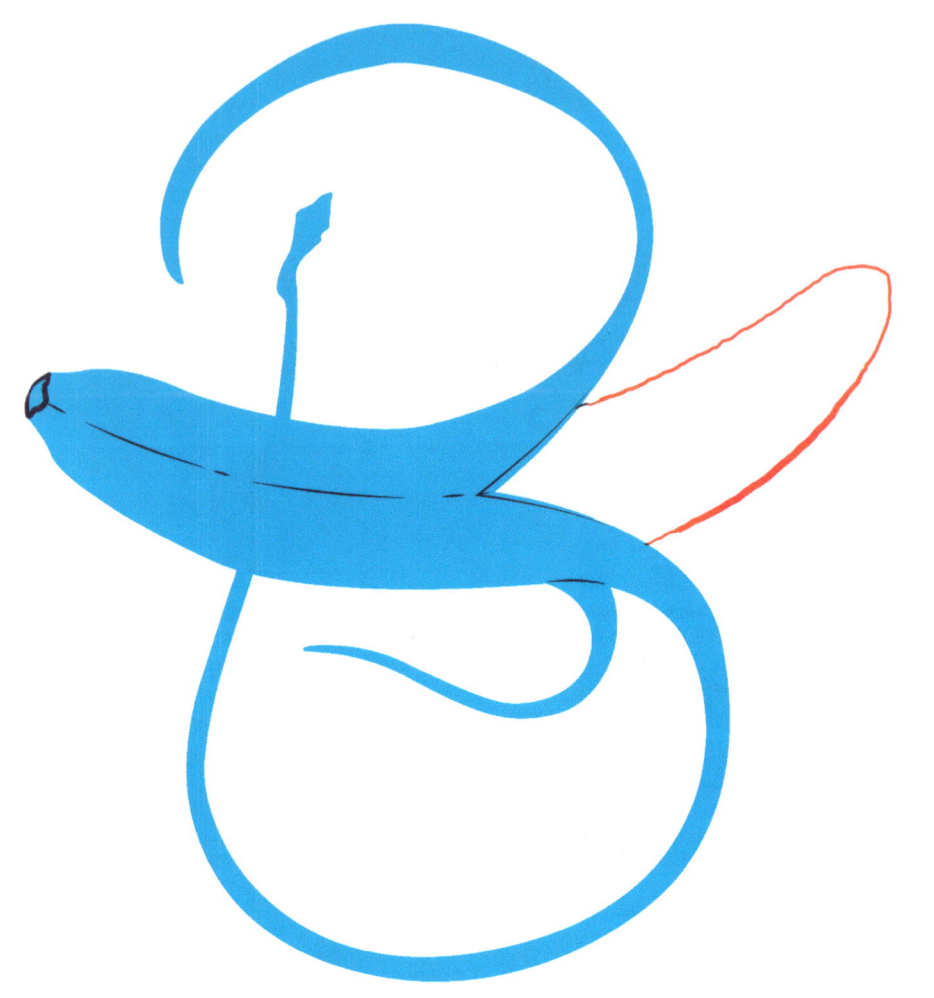

Banana

Paul Conrad
pconrad.1@go.ccad.edu

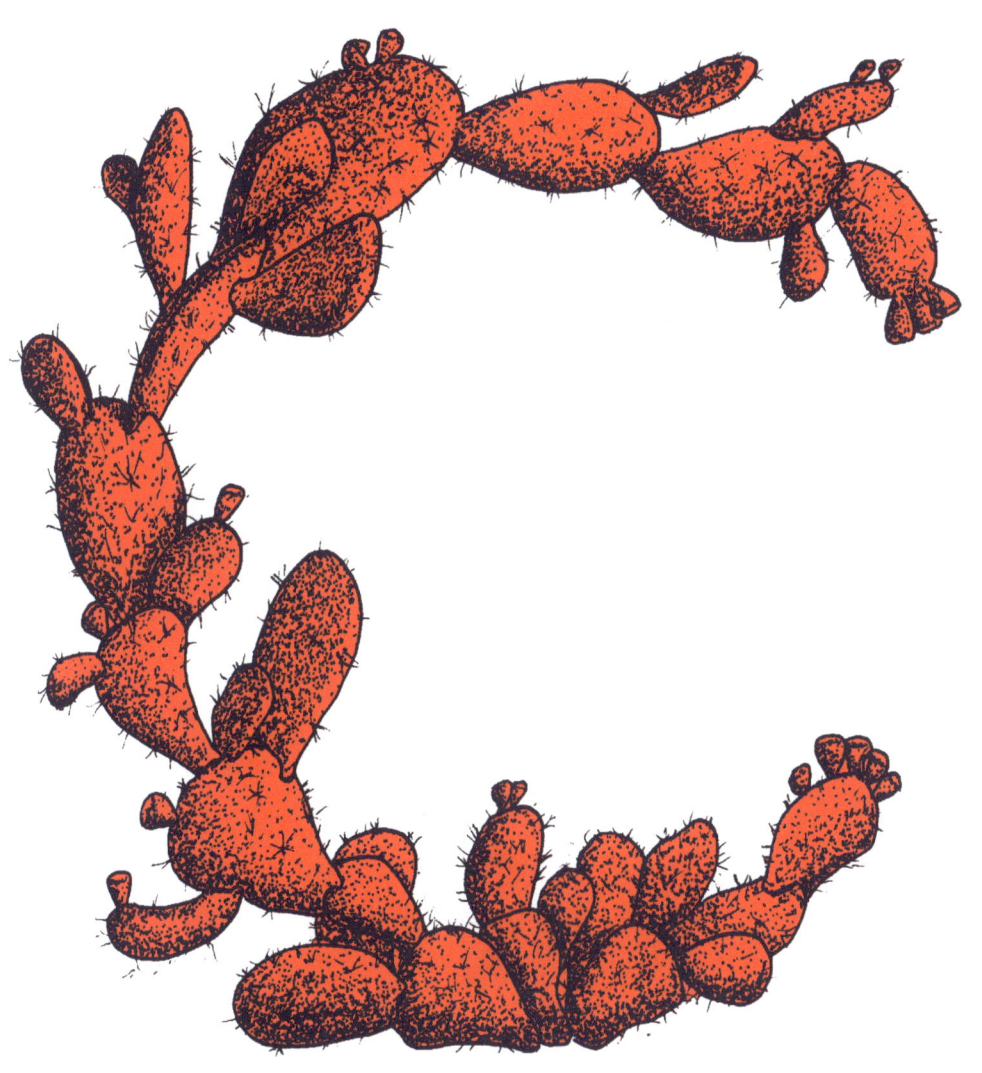

Cactus

Logan Hamblin
lhamblin-willis.1@go.ccad.edu

DUTCH SHEPHERD

Hope Taylor
kmkarma6@yahoo.com

ELECTRIC EEL

Karl Fekete
fekete.karl@gmail.com

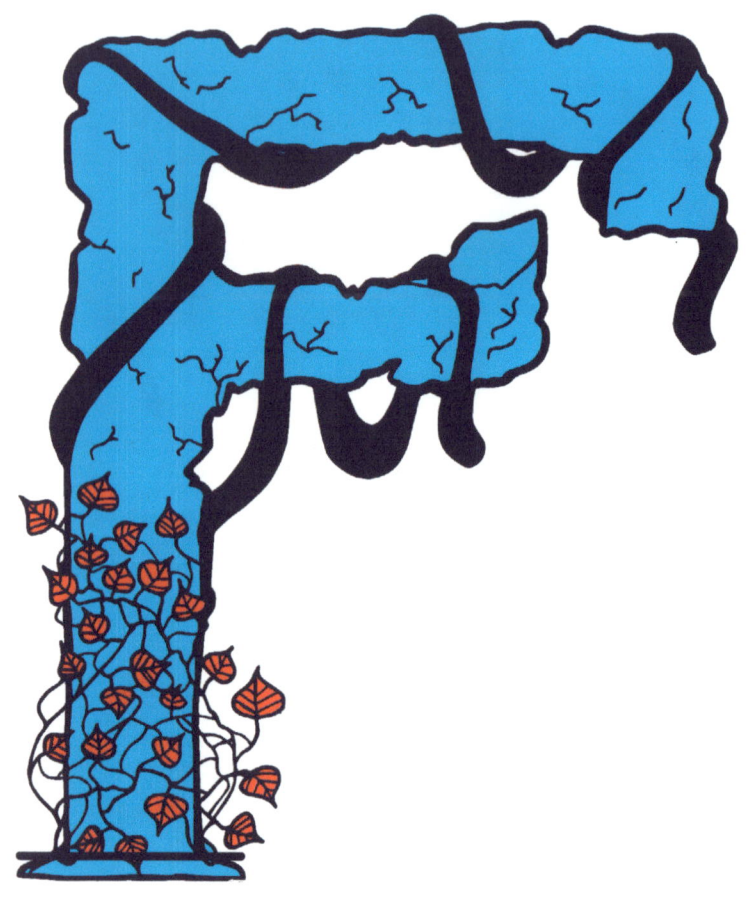

FERN

Dylan Schiff
dschiff.1@go.ccad.edu

GALÁPAGOS TORTOISE

James Carpenter
jamesfreelances@gmail.com

Huckleberry

Jennifer Hammock
jenniferhammock@yahoo.com

ISCHIUM

Celia Swetland
cswetland.1@go.ccad.edu

JACKALOPE

Samuel Harachis
sharachis.1@go.ccad.edu

KANGAROO

Kyle Kennedy
kennedy343@hotmail.com

LADYBUG

Paul Conrad
pconrad.1@go.ccad.edu

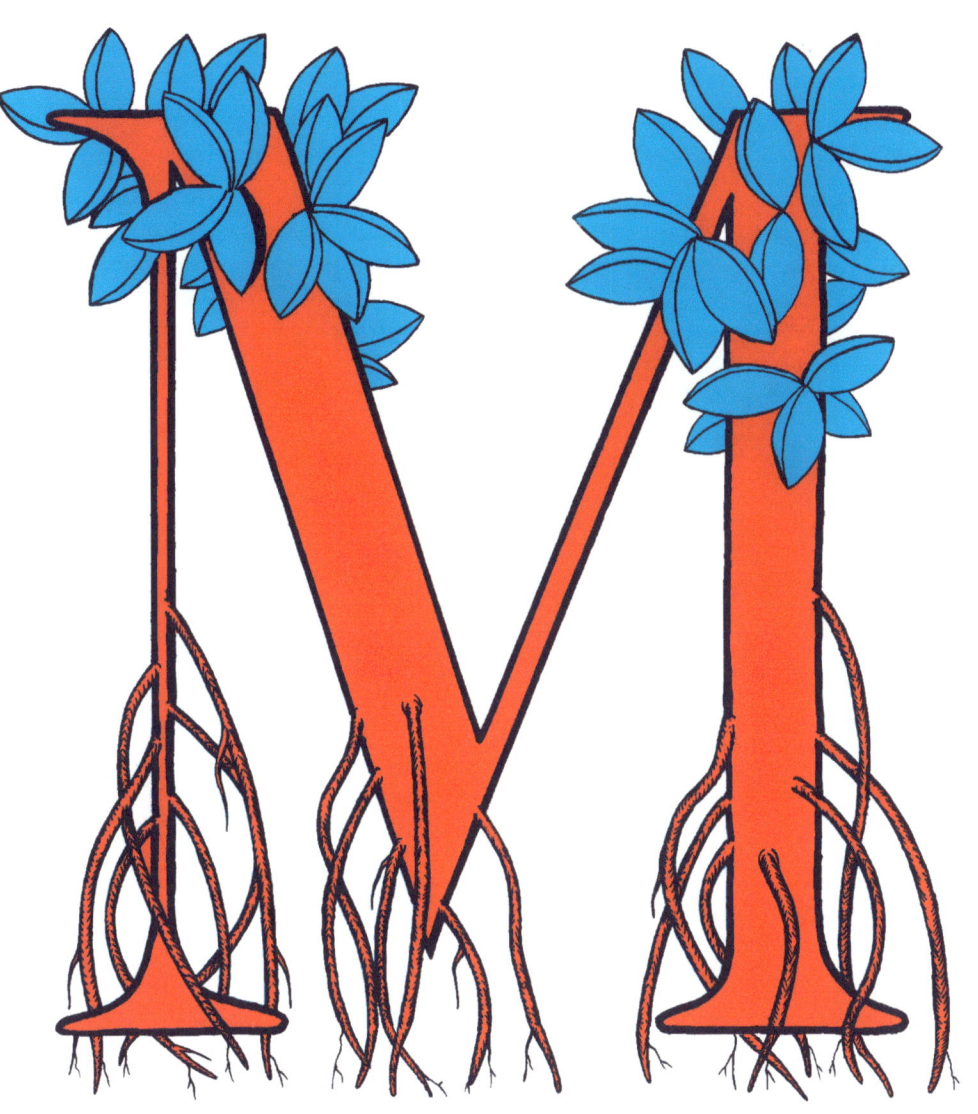

Mangrove

Paul Conrad
pconrad.1@go.ccad.edu

*N*ASTURTIUM

Grace Cole
graceanne.design@gmail.com

*O*CTOPUS

Paul Conrad
pconrad.1@go.ccad.edu

PEACOCK

Rachel Giardina
giardina_rachel@yahoo.com

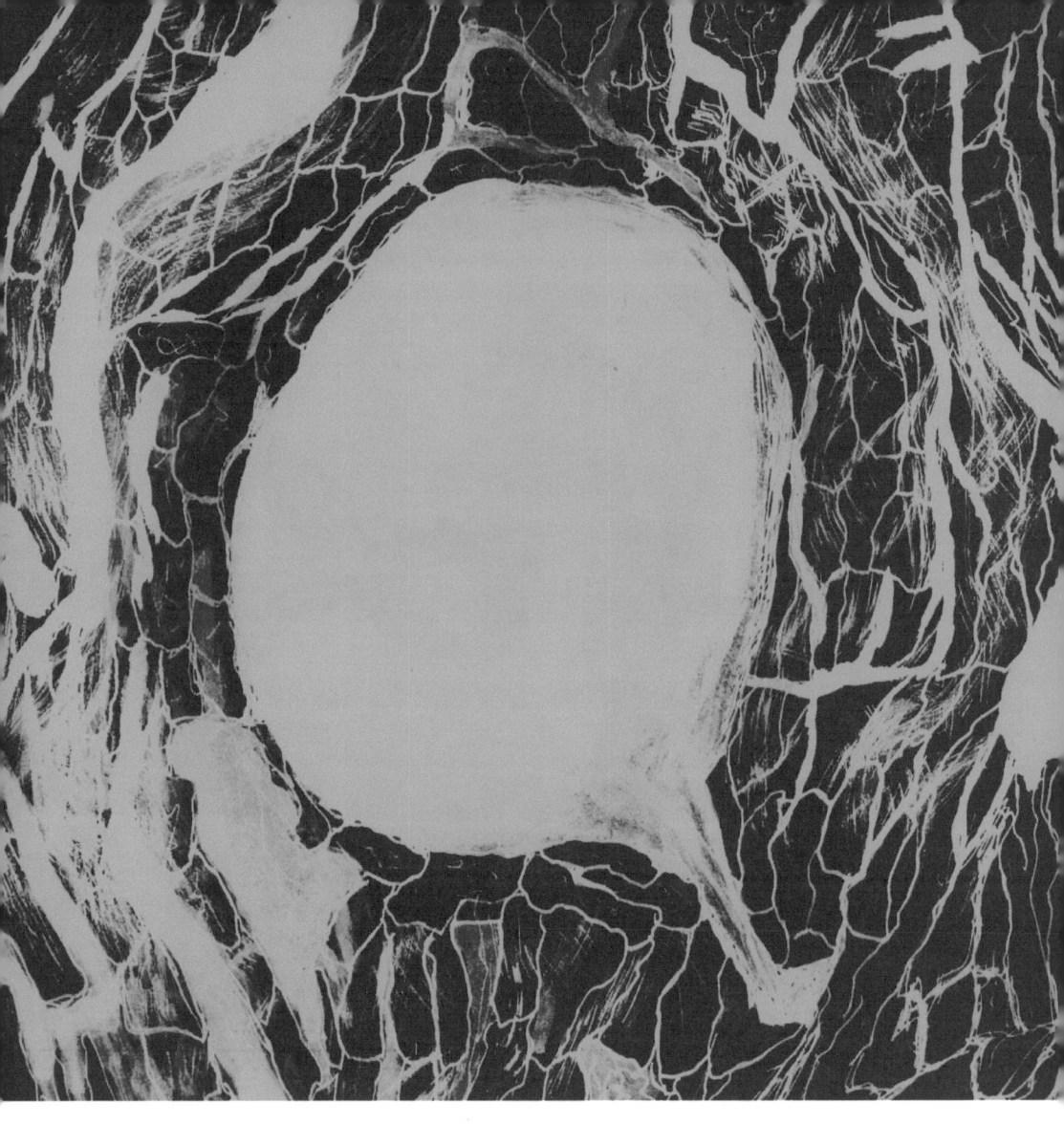

QUERCUS ROBUR

Logan Hamblin
lhamblin-willis.1@go.ccad.edu

ROSE

Karl Fekete
fekete.karl@gmail.com

SPIDER

Jennifer Hammock
jenniferhammock@yahoo.com

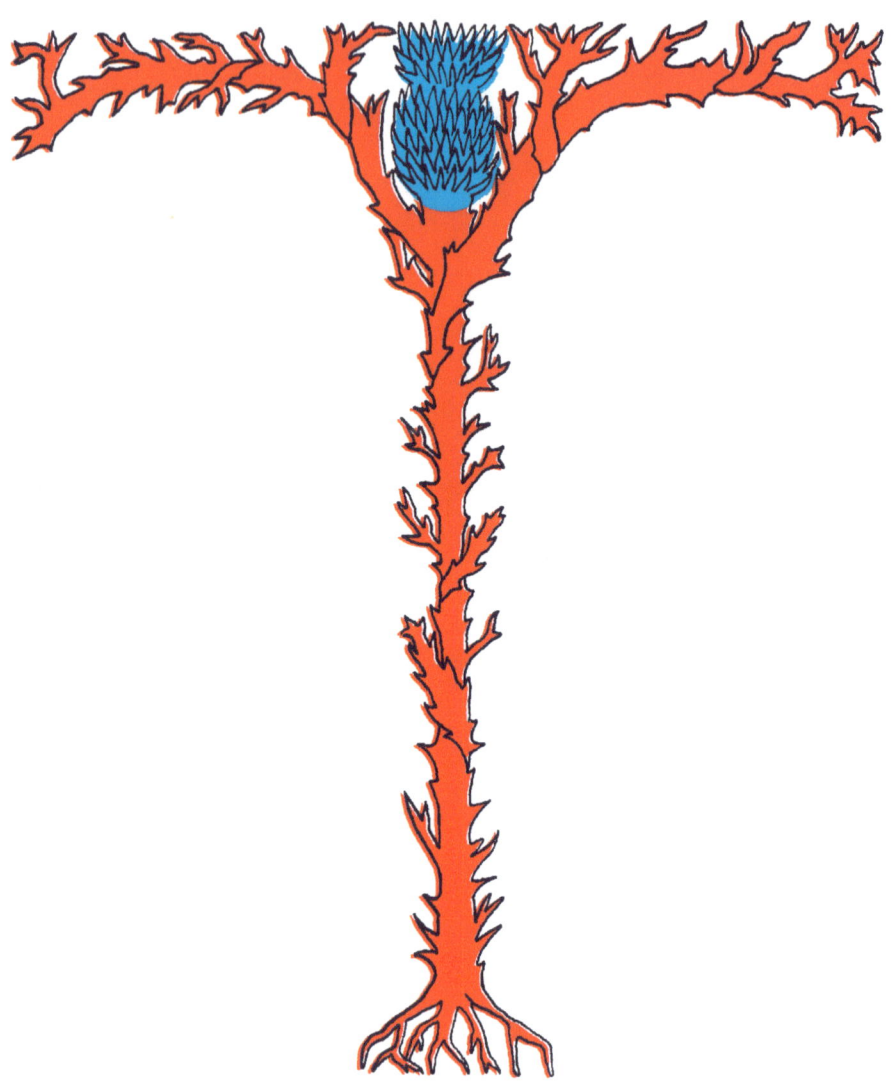

THISTLE

Connor Luft
cluft.1@go.ccad.edu

URIGINIA

James Carpenter
jamesfreelances@gmail.com

VISERION

Nate Guerra
brotherbeard@gmail.com

WOODPECKER

Marissa Ohm
mohm.1@go.ccad.edu

$\mathcal{X}\gamma LOSM$

Patrick Cantwell

pcantwell.1@go.ccad.edu

YELLOW TAIL

Nate Guerra
brotherbeard@gmail.com

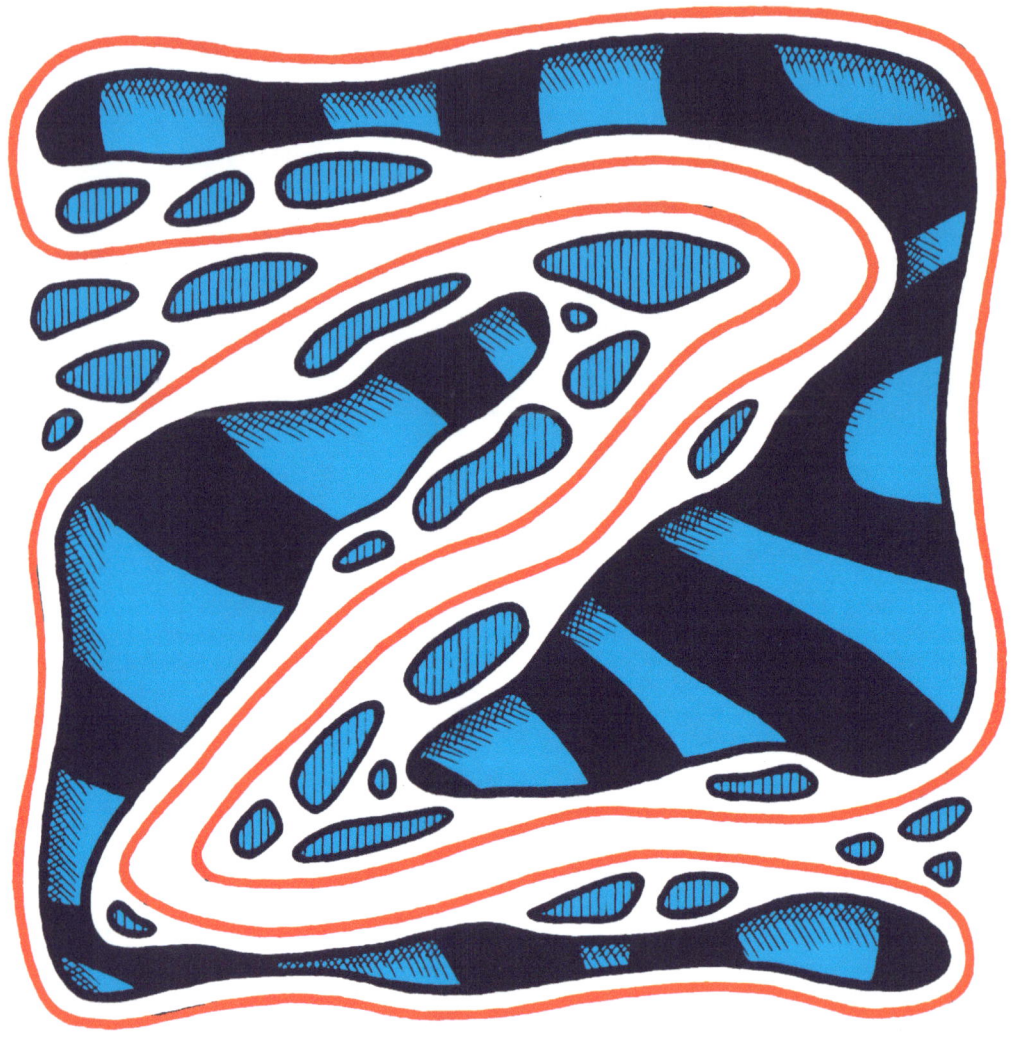

ZEBRA

Patrick Cantwell
pcantwell.1@go.ccad.edu

JAMES CARPENTER • I'm a design student because it is the most challenging and rewarding career I could ever dream of. For the rest of my life I get to solve problems, influence strangers, be creative, and love my job.
www.behance.net/JamesCarpenter

GRACE COLE • Typography is one of those areas of design that I'm sure all students love and hate at the same time. It is a balancing act. So right now, my favorite thing about typography is seeing how experienced designers have handled it. There's a learning curve in spotting the difference between successful and unsuccessful type treatments and then being able to say why. There is just so much to learn and that is both humbling and inspiring.
www.behance.net/GraceCole

PAUL CONRAD • Anyone can create their own style of lettering and call it their own. I like how the way a letter is shaped can indicate a certain mood or meaning. The ambition to get a job, keeping up with peers, and the incentive to do good in school is what inspires me the most. You can never learn everything about design, so it's a fun adventure.
pconrad.1@go.ccad.edu

KARL FEKETE • Typography and lettering are my favorite things within the realm of design. They provide such a fulfilling outlet for me, since language and alphabets are so relatable. It is something that we all have in common, and there is a never-ending wealth of uses for typography, and illustration allows a limitless expanse of what you can do with an alphabet. Every single letter has been designed and illustrated millions of times over, and there are still new solutions popping up daily.
www.koolkarl.com

RACHEL GIARDINA • The best part about being a designer is that I am able to create something that's different and out of the ordinary. I am able to express myself through my work. My favorite thing about typography is I can design a letter to match the style of a mood or theme.
www.behance.net/rachelgiardina

 **NATE GUERRA** • Who inspires me to do my best work? My brother passed away a few years ago; he was one of my biggest supports. I push forward everyday for him and for my family members who were never able to accomplish the things I have. They inspire me and keep me on my toes. *www.brotherbeard.com*

 **JENNIFER HAMMOCK** • Inspiration comes from the lines in an automobile to the texture of a tree. Even the mood you are in at the time you are creating something has a profound effect on the outcome. Everything around you is inspiration whether you realize it or not. My family drives me to be a better designer and speak through my design. *jenniferhammock@yahoo.com*

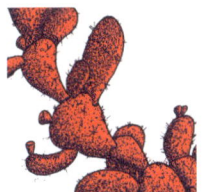 **LOGAN N. HAMBLIN** • In my work, the best inspiration comes from the past. Old typography, advertising, patterns, colors, cinema (especially horror and sci-fi), and of course artwork all inspire me heavily. I also love mid-century modern design because it's the perfect blend of modernism, futurism, and functionality. I really enjoy reflecting the past in my design and also my artwork when and where ever I can. I have a lot of respect for the past, and in my opinion sometimes older is, in fact, better. *lhamblin-willis.1@go.ccad.edu*

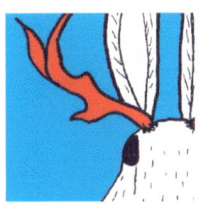 **SAMUEL HARACHIS** • My family are my best critics. They are helpful when I struggle with ideas and I can trust them to give me their honest opinions or suggestions that will make me look at things in a different perspective. *sharachis.1@go.ccad.edu*

 **KYLE KENNEDY** • I enjoy executing the design and adding color after figuring out the concept and what the style is going to look like. Hearing the reaction of what viewers see and interpret is what I enjoy most about the end result of designing. What drives me to improve my work is seeing what designers and my peers create allowing me to reflect on my own work and try something different. *kennedy343@hotmail.com*

CONNOR LUFT • A designer can make the world a little bit more pleasant just through visual aesthetics. Putting something beautiful out there and being able to call it your job is such a satisfying feeling. I work through inspiration that is all around me: nature, music, books, brands. The list could go on. I remember once I was at the grocery store, and I found some packaging for cheese that I just loved. I was so inspired that I ran home without finishing my shopping and got to work drawing out type. I didn't know what I was going to do, but I was sure gonna do it! That's exactly how I work best—I get inspired and I dive right in. *www.behance.net/connorluft*

CANDICE OATES • I am incredibly intrigued by typography. My favorite thing about it is definitely its history and what we can do with typography today. In the past, type has always been structured and made to look clean and orderly and it never strayed from a straight line. And now... well, I mean, we're making letters into plants and animals! *COates.1@go.ccad.edu*

MARISSA OHM • I know that when I make something it is different than my last and that every work is unique in its own way. Design is also everywhere and is influential, which motivates me to try and make my work count. It is interesting to see all the different ways that designers can go with different kinds of fonts. I also find it interesting that people can have an insight on a word even if they don't speak that language at least that is how I feel when I look at design from other countries; I may not know what it says but how the type looks can have a huge impact on my first impression. *MOhm.1@go.ccad.edu*

CELIA SWETLAND • It is always a fun challenge to design and think of new ways you could design the word/letter. I also like that it could be a basic letter/word form or you could make it completely an illustrational form with the letter some how incorporated into it. What inspires me when it comes to my work is what I see in my everyday life, I defiantly believe that you are influenced by your surroundings and things that you are interested in. *behance.net/CeliaSwetland*

DYLAN SCHIFF • There are so many different ways to be creative with typography. There are no boundaries of what you can do with the shapes that make up a letter. I also love the challenge of giving the type a personality corresponding to the rest of the design. I get most of my inspiration from the world around me so I try to make it a point to be overly observant of my surroundings. You never know how or when a great idea will be born! *www.behance.net/DylanSchiff*

HOPE TAYLOR • I love seeing how simple I can make something and still be able to convey the idea, message, or brand or whatever I'm working on. Using different type treatments can give words an entirely different mood and feeling. I also love being able to convey what I'm trying to say just through the visual clues of type treatment. *behance.net/hopetaylor*

PATRICK CANTWELL • My favorite thing about typography is the limitless options and applications that can be created from it. I am inspired by friends, family, and the internet. And nature. And trees. *www.behance.net/patrickcantwell*

www.ingramcontent.com/pod-product-compliance
Lightning Source LLC
Chambersburg PA
CBHW040327010626
45792CB00024B/2178